DRAW SUPERHEROES

in 4 Easy Steps

Then Write a Story

BOOM

1

2

3

4

Enslow Elementary
an imprint of
Enslow Publishers, Inc.
40 Industrial Road
Box 398
Berkeley Heights, NJ 07922
USA

http://www.enslow.com

Stephanie LaBaff
Illustrated by Tom LaBaff

Enslow Elementary, an imprint of Enslow Publishers, Inc.

Enslow Elementary® is a registered trademark of Enslow Publishers, Inc.

Library of Congress Cataloging-in-Publication Data
LaBaff, Stephanie.
  Draw superheroes in 4 easy steps : then write a story / Stephanie LaBaff.
      p. cm. — (Drawing in 4 easy steps)
  Includes index.
  Summary: "Learn to draw superheroes, and write a story about them, with a story example and story prompts"—Provided by publisher.
  ISBN 978-0-7660-3842-4
  1. Superheroes in art—Juvenile literature. 2. Figure drawing—Technique—Juvenile litera-
ture. 3. Superhero comic books, strips, etc.—Authorship—
Juvenile literature. I. Title. II. Title: Draw superheroes in four easy steps.
  NC1764.8.H47L33 2012
  743.4—dc22
                              2011017566
Paperback ISBN 978-1-4644-0015-5
ePUB ISBN 978-1-4645-0464-8
PDF ISBN 978-1-4646-0464-5

Printed in the United States of America

092011 Lake Book Manufacturing, Inc., Melrose Park, IL

10 9 8 7 6 5 4 3 2 1

Illustration Credits: Tom LaBaff

Contents

Getting Started

Lots of Paper

Pencil sharpener

your imagination

← Pencil

Eraser

ARTIST'S SURVIVAL KIT

Drawing superheroes is as easy as 1, 2, 3, 4! Follow the 4 steps for each picture in this book. You will be amazed at what you can draw. After some practice, you will be able to make your own adjustments, too. Change a pose, move a leg, or draw a different hero. There are lots of possibilities!

Follow the 4 Steps

1 Start with big shapes, such as the body.

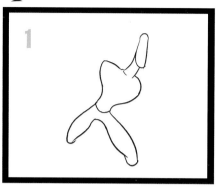

2 Add smaller shapes, such as the arms and feet. In each step, new lines are shown in red.

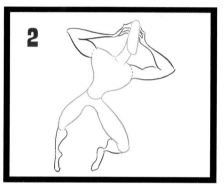

3 Continue adding new lines. Erase lines as needed.

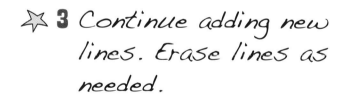

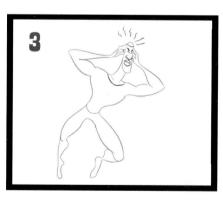

4 Add final details and color. Your superhero will come to life!

Amp

1

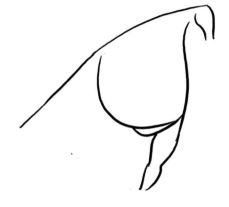

2

Erase the dotted
line behind the
head.

3

Aquamy

1

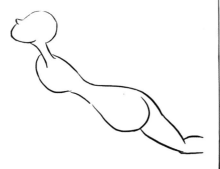

2

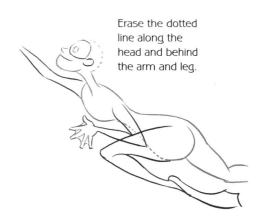

Erase the dotted line along the head and behind the arm and leg.

3

Erase the dotted line behind her elbow.

4

Cinder

1

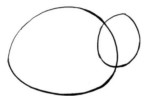

Keep the oval and
the circle loose.

2

Erase the dotted line
behind the head, arm,
and leg.

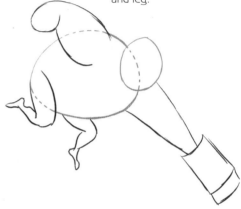

3

Erase the dotted
line behind the
hand and neck.

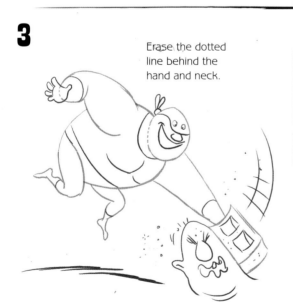

4

Auggie

1

2

Erase the dotted line behind the arms, neck, and foot.

3

4

Fuego

1

2

Erase the dotted line behind the head.

3

4

Blackpowder

1

The body is a
figure 8 shape.

2

Erase the dotted line at the
shoulder and behind the leg.

3

4

Icer

1

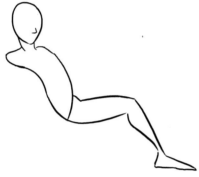

2

Erase the dotted line at the shoulder.

3

4

Conformer

1

2

Erase the dotted line along the right shoulder.

3

4

Jet

1

2

3

Erase the dotted line behind the head and arm.

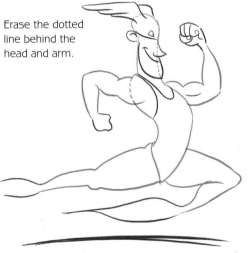

4

Ivy

1

Think of a peanut with legs.

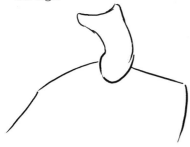

2

Erase the dotted line behind the neck and shoulders.

3

4

Mindfreak

1

2

Erase the dotted line at the shoulders.

3

4

Lovey

1

2

Erase the dotted
line behind the leg
and shoulders.

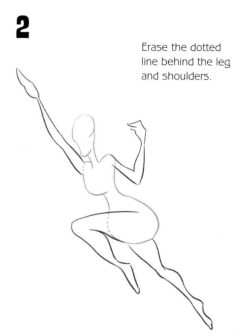

3

Erase the dotted line
behind the head.

4

Mortar

1

2

Erase the dotted line behind the head.

3

4

SNAP

Puttygirl

1

2

Erase the dotted line
at the shoulders.

3

4

Nox

1

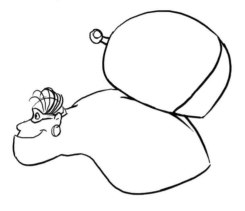

2

3

Erase the dotted line behind the tank and arm.

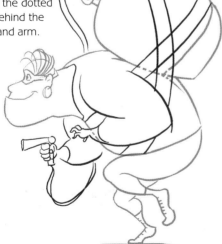

4

Shadow

1

2

3

Erase the dotted line at the shoulders.

4

Puddles

1

2

3

Erase the dotted line behind the knee and his right thumb.

4

22

Sandblaster

1

2

Erase the dotted line behind the head.

3

Erase the dotted line behind the shoulder.

4

Weatherman

1

2

Erase the dotted line
behind the neck.

3

Erase the dotted line
at the shoulders.

4

Whip

1

2

Erase the dotted line behind the neck and leg.

3

Erase the dotted line at the shoulders and behind the head.

Think of a lion's tail when you make the arms.

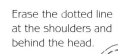

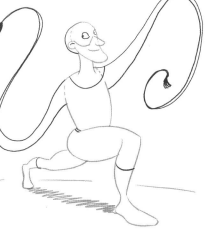

4

Armor

1

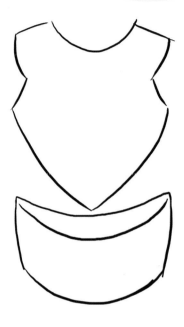

2

3

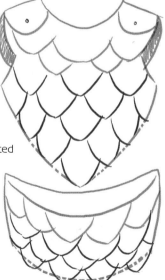

Erase the dotted line along the bottom of both pieces.

4

Fire

1

Make loose,
wispy lines.

2

3

4

Glove

1

2

Erase the dotted line
behind the finger and
thumb.

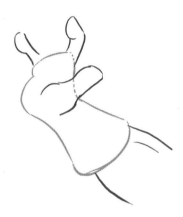

3

4

Magic Crystal

1

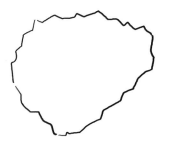

2

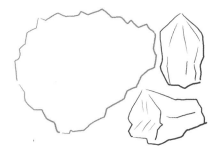

3

4

Lantern

1

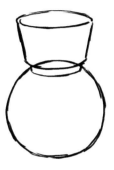

2

Erase the dotted
line behind the
top of the globe.

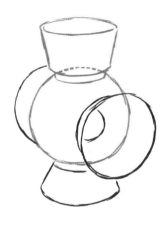

3

4

Laser

1

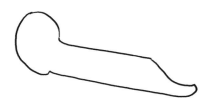

2

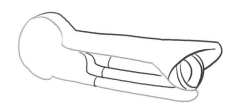

3

Erase the dotted
line behind the
circles.

4

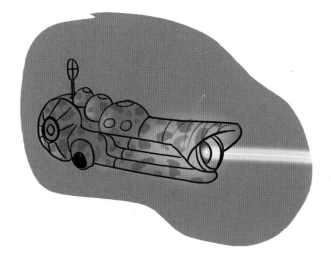

Amethyst

1

2

3

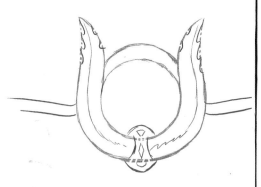

Erase the dotted
line behind the
medallion.

4

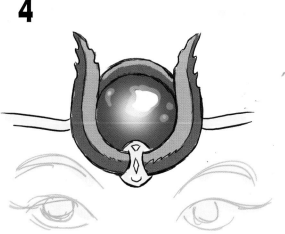

Shields

1

Don't worry about making a perfect circle. Keep it sketchy!

2

3

Put your own design in the center.

4

Add some battle scars for fun.

Star

1

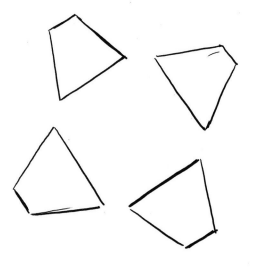

2

Erase the dotted lines on the arms of the star.

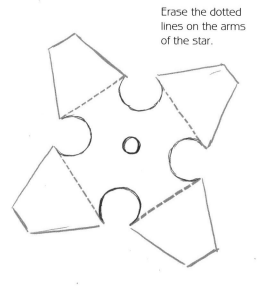

3

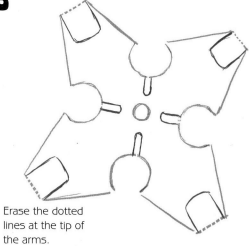

Erase the dotted lines at the tip of the arms.

4

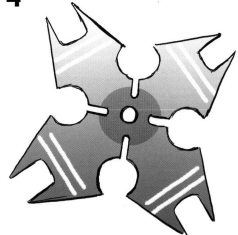

Steel

1

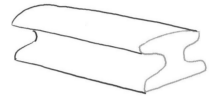

2

3

4

How to Write a Story

Write a Story in 5 Easy Steps

Are you ready to write a story to go with your drawings? Maybe you have a story you want to illustrate. Follow these five simple steps to make your very own story with drawings.

Step 1: *Prewriting*

Do you want to write about superheroes? Maybe you have an idea for a story about superheroes. Keep in mind the drawings you want to use and base your story around them.

One way to begin your story is to
answer these questions: Who? What?
Why? Where? When? How?
For example:
Who is your superhero?
What happens to him in your story?
Why is his story interesting?
Where and when does he live?
How does he use his superpowers?

    Here is a good brainstorming exercise.
Fold a paper into six columns. Write the
words *Who? What? Why? Where? When?*
and *How?* at the top of each column. Write
down every answer that comes into your
head in the matching column. Do this for
about five or ten minutes. Take a look at your
list and pick out the ideas that you like the
best. Now you are ready to write your story.

Superhero Story Starters

Just as the plane was about to crash, the
     superhero swooped in . . .

There was a loud cracking sound and
     then . . . BOOM!

The children were trapped in the car
     as it was swept down the river . . .

The evil scientist was about to blow up
     the lab when . . .

The world was about to end. Nothing
     could save the planet. unless . . .

The superheroes worked together against
     the invaders . . .

Step 2: Writing

Use the ideas from the list you made in Step 1. Write your story all the way through. Don't stop to make changes. You can always make changes later.

A story about a superhero who sleeps through a crisis isn't very interesting. What could happen to this superhero? What if a boat full of people was sinking? Think of all the things that could go wrong. Your story will be more exciting if you don't make things too easy for the superhero.

Step 3: *Editing*

Read your story. Is there a way to make it better? Rewrite the parts that you can improve. You might want to ask a friend or teacher to help. Ask them for their ideas.

Step 4: *Proofreading*

Make sure the spelling, punctuation, and grammar are correct.

Storyboarding

Check to see that your story works with your drawings. Find a table or other flat surface. Spread your drawings out in the order that goes with your story. Then place the matching text below each drawing. When you have your story the way you like it, go to Step 5. You can pick a way to publish your story.

Step 5: *Publishing Your Book*

You can make your story into a book. There are many different forms your book can take. Here are a few ideas:

⭐ Simple book – Staple sheets of blank paper together along their edges.

⭐ Folded book – Fold sheets of blank paper in half, then staple on the fold.

⭐ Hardcover book – Buy a blank hardcover book. Then write your finished story in the book, leaving spaces to add your art.

⭐ Bound book – Punch a few holes along the edges of some pieces of paper. Tie them up or fill the holes with paper fasteners. There are many fun and colorful binding options at office supply stores.

✯ Digital book – Create a digital book using your computer. There are some great programs available. Ask an adult to help you find one that is right for you.

Our Story

You have finished the five steps of writing and illustrating a story. We bet you created a great story! Want to see ours? Turn the page and take a peek.

Supers to the Rescue

The Supers were all talking at once. Ivy whistled to quiet them down. "Listen up, everybody! We aren't going to figure anything out if we can't hear each other. We have to find out what's happened to Icer and Puddles."

The superheroes had a big problem. That was nothing new—solving tough problems was their job. But this time it was personal. Two of their own had gone missing overnight.

Mortar took charge. "Lovey, you're our fastest flyer. Start flying around the area and see if you spot any clues from the air."

Lovey sprang up and shot out the door. In a few minutes, she was back with news.

"There's a path of water leading from this building straight out to the desert. It can only be from Puddles!" Everyone knew Puddles left a trail of water wherever he went. "Let's go, team!"

The superheroes charged out to follow the trail, some on foot and some by air. Soon they were out in the desert, where the path of water led into a dark cave.

"Icer and Puddles must be in there," said Weatherman.

"Right," said Ivy. "And whoever took them is probably dangerous, so we need to be careful. Shadow can sneak into the cave without being seen."

Shadow tiptoed into the cave, deep into the darkness. Finally she turned a corner and found herself in front of a giant ring of fire. Above the fire, in a hanging cage, were Icer and Puddles. And in the center of it all stood Fuego, their archenemy. He spoke to his prisoners.

"Soon all your water powers will be dried up! And I will be unstoppable!" Shadow ran back to report to the others.

"I think I can help!" said Weatherman. "Let's move!" The group entered the cave again, and as they approached the fire, Weatherman used his powers to stir up a giant rain cloud. The rain poured down on the fire and Fuego, drenching them both. Fuego tried to run, but Ivy used her long stems to tie him up. Lovey flew up to the cage and freed Icer and Puddles.

"This isn't over yet!" cried Fuego. "Someday I will be the most powerful force in the world!" he cried:

"Sorry, Fuego," laughed Lovey. "But I'm afraid you're all wet!"

Further Reading

Books

Hart, Christopher. *Superheroes and Beyond*. New York: Crown Publishing Group, 2009.

Reynolds, Aaron. *Superhero School*. New York: Bloomsbury Publishing, 2009.

Shalant, Phyllis. *Society of Super Secret Superheroes: The Great Cape Rescue*. New York: Penguin, 2007.

Walter Foster Publising. *Learn to Draw Your Favorite Disney Pixar Characters*. Mankato, Minn.: Black Rabbit Books, 2010.

Weitzman, Jacqueline Preiss. *Superhero Joe*. New York: Simon and Schuster, 2011.

Internet Addresses

Marvel. Create Your Own Superhero Gallery. 2011.
<http://marvel.com/games/cyos>
Superhero Network. Superhero Database. 2012.
<http://www.superherodb.com>
Wikipedia. Superhuman Features. 2011.
<http://en.wikipedia.org/wiki/List_of_superhuman_features_and_abilities_in_fiction>

Index